Camping Recipes:

Foil Packet Cooking

100 Foil Packet Recipes for Campfires and Grills

Bonnie Scott

BONNIE SCOTT

ISBN-13: 978-1490980584

2

CONTENTS

Foil Packet Tips

- Don't be frugal with the amount of foil to be used for each packet. It is better to have too much foil than not enough foil; you don't want your food to spill down into the fire. Too much foil can always be folded over.

- Spraying the foil with non-stick cooking spray like Pam works wonders. Sometimes the food still sticks to the foil, but will easily be removed with gentle prodding.

- The best foil to use for outdoor cooking is heavy duty aluminum foil. If only standard aluminum foil is available, use 2 or more thicknesses of foil for each packet.

- Always put the meat on the bottom when adding your ingredients because meats will take the longest to cook.

- Place the packets on hot coals or a campfire grill, not directly in the fire itself. Charcoal will take about 30 minutes to be ready for cooking.

- Rotate the packets 1/4 turn a couple of times during cooking. Open the packet and check the food when it should be finished cooking, being careful of the steam.

- Cut all the vegetables to be about the same size so they will cook evenly.

- When food is cooked, open one end of the foil packet carefully or cut a large X across the top of each one to allow steam to escape; open top or fold back foil.

- Remember that campfires and grills will vary in heat, so it is best to check with a meat thermometer for safe cooking.

- The USDA recommends the following internal temperatures as a minimum for a safe temperature. This is not necessarily the degree of doneness you want for your food; it is merely the minimum internal temperature. After the food reaches the safe minimum temperature, determine how much longer to cook the food for optimum flavor. Please refer to the USDA chart on the next page.

    For example:

  Beef: Cook ground beef, hamburgers to 160 degrees F.

  Roasts and steaks – 145 degrees F for rare, 160 degrees F for medium and 175 degrees F for well done.

Safe Minimum Internal Temperature Chart

Food	°F
Ground Meat & Meat Mixtures	
Beef, Pork, Veal, Lamb	160
Turkey, Chicken	165
Fresh Beef, Pork, Veal, Lamb	
Steaks, roasts, chops	145 *
Ham	
Fresh (raw)	145 *
Precooked (to reheat)	140

* as measured with a food thermometer before removing meat from the heat source. For safety and quality, allow meat to rest for at least three minutes before carving or consuming. For reasons of personal preference, consumers may choose to cook meat to higher temperatures.

Poultry	
Chicken and Turkey, whole	165
Poultry pieces	165
Duck & Goose	165
Stuffing (cooked alone or in bird)	165

Chart reprinted from
http://www.fsis.usda.gov/wps/portal/fsis/topics/food-safety-education/get-answers/food-safety-fact-sheets/safe-food-handling/kitchen-companion-your-safe-food-handbook/ct_index

Flat Packets

The flat packet is best to cook **meat and fish**. The flat packet doesn't allow for as much steam as the tent packet and meat and fish require browning rather than steaming.

1. For each packet, tear off a piece of heavy duty foil 18" x 18" or the size the recipe designates. If you are using standard aluminum foil, double or triple the sheets.

2. Spray the foil with non-stick cooking spray. It doesn't matter which side of the foil you place the ingredients in – either the shiny side or dull side will work fine.

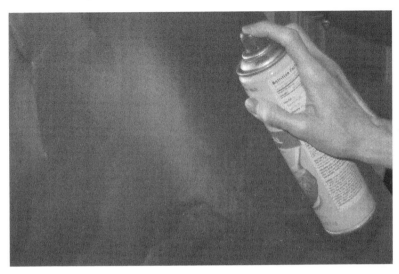

3. Place the prepared ingredients in the center of the foil.

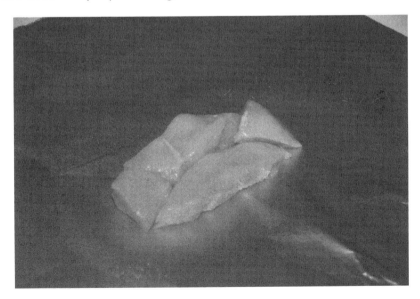

4. Grab each of the longer sides and bring them together in the center of the packet.

5. Fold the edges of the long sides together. Tightly fold them again several times and crimp well.

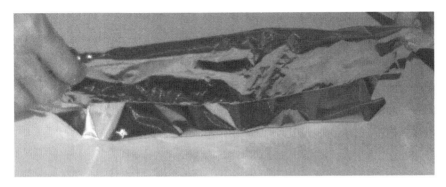

Keep folding until the foil is flat against the food.

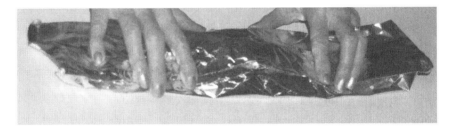

6. Fold each short end over and crimp well. Keep folding the short ends until they also reach the food.

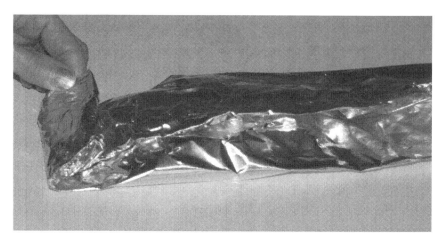

Tent Packets

Tent packets are best used to cook **vegetables or fruits and meats combined with vegetables**. The tent packet allows for more steam to circulate through the packet.

1. Tear off a piece of heavy duty foil 18" x 24" or the size the recipe designates, for each packet. The foil should be at least twice as long as the ingredients you are wrapping up. If you are using standard aluminum foil, double or triple the sheets.

2. Spray the foil with non-stick cooking spray.

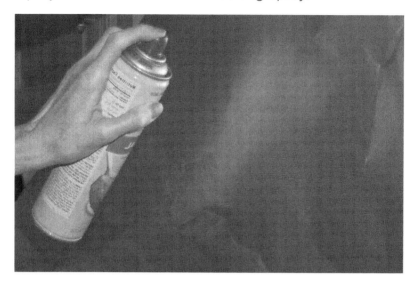

3. Place the prepared ingredients in the center of the foil.

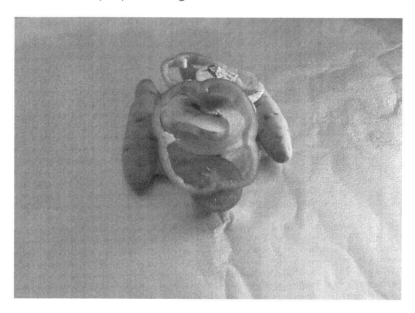

4. Grab each of the longer sides and bring them together in the center of the packet.

5. Fold the edges of the long sides together, folding over about an inch.

For the "tent", leave several inches of air space between the foil and the food - hence the term "tent". Tightly crimp the edges and fold the edges again if need be until only 2 or 3 inches of space is in the packet.

6. Fold each short end over and crimp well. Don't roll them up tight to the food - leave one or two inches of space between the end of the fold and the food.

Foil Packets in the Oven

Foil packets can also be cooked in the oven. Nice to know when you make the packets up for grilling and unknowingly, your grill is out of gas. Just cook the packets in the oven at about twice the time you would cook them on a covered grill. Place packets on a cookie sheet for ease of handling.

The temperature conversion from grill to oven is:

Medium Heat on Grill   = 375 degrees F in the oven

Medium High Heat on Grill = 400 degrees F in the oven

High Heat on Grill   = 425 degrees F in the oven

Chicken

Oriental Chicken

4 chicken breasts, boneless and skinless
1/2 cup sweet and sour sauce
1 can pineapple chunks, 8 oz., drained
1/2 bell pepper, cut into thin strips
1/4 onion, cut into wedges
1/2 cup chow mein noodles
Heavy duty aluminum foil – 4 pieces 18" x 18"

Spray each piece foil with non-stick cooking spray. Place one chicken breast in the center of each foil and top with one tablespoon of sweet and sour sauce and 1/4 of the pineapple chunks. Add 1/4 of the pepper strips and onion wedges. Top off with the remaining sweet and sour sauce.

Fold the foil loosely over veggies and chicken to form a tent packet, folding and crimping seams tightly.

Rotate packets 1/2 turn every 10 minutes on the grill. When done, place a portion of chow mein noodles on top of the ingredients in each packet and serve. Yield: 4 servings.

COOKING

Place foil packet on hot coals or a campfire grill for 30 to 40 minutes.

Or place foil packet in covered grill on medium-low heat for 15 to 22 minutes.

Spicy Jerk Wings

6 chicken wings, split
4 tablespoons jerk seasoning
2 tablespoons vegetable oil
1/4 cup cilantro, chopped
3 lemon wedges
Heavy duty aluminum foil - 18" x 24"

Combine the jerk seasoning and oil and coat the chicken with mixture. Spray foil with non-stick cooking spray. Place the wings in the center of foil and pour remaining mixture over them.

Fold the foil loosely to create a tent packet, folding and crimping seams tightly. Place over hot coals, rotating 1/4 turn at half done. When wings are cooked, sprinkle cilantro on them and serve with lemons.

COOKING

Place foil packet on hot coals or a campfire grill for 25 minutes.

Or place foil packet in uncovered grill on medium heat for 25 minutes.

Tropical Chicken

3 chicken breasts, bone-in
3 slices pineapple, drained
1/2 cup slivered almonds
1/4 teaspoon rosemary
1/4 teaspoon tarragon
Salt and pepper to taste
Heavy duty aluminum foil – 3 pieces of 18" x 24"

Spray foil with non-stick cooking spray. Brown chicken lightly in butter and place each chicken breast in the center of a piece of foil. In same skillet, brown 3 slices of pineapple and 1/2 cup slivered almonds. Divide evenly and arrange over each chicken breast. Sprinkle each chicken with salt, pepper, rosemary and tarragon – either fresh or dried.

Fold the foil tightly to form a flat packet, crimping seams securely. Cook using one of the options below. Yield: 3 servings.

COOKING

Place foil packet on hot coals or a campfire grill for 30 to 45 minutes.

Or place foil packet in covered grill on medium-low heat for 22 to 25 minutes.

Chicken in the Garden

4 chicken breasts, boneless and skinless
8 small potatoes (or 2 baking potatoes, peeled and cut in fourths)
8 small tomatoes
4 slices of onion
8 large mushroom slices
8 green pepper rings, sliced
4 teaspoons Worcestershire sauce
Salt and pepper to taste
1/4 teaspoon paprika
4 tablespoons butter
Heavy duty aluminum foil – 4 pieces of 18" x 24"

Cut each chicken breast into 2 pieces. Any pieces of chicken that are an inch thick or more, cut again. Spray foil with non-stick cooking spray.

In each of the four pieces of foil, layer 2 cut up pieces of chicken, 2 potatoes, 2 tomatoes, 1 onion slice, 2 mushroom slices, 2 green pepper rings, 1 teaspoon Worcestershire sauce, and sprinkle with salt, pepper and paprika. Dot with 1 tablespoon butter.

 Fold the foil loosely to form a tent packet, folding and crimping seams tightly. Cook until chicken is opaque and the potatoes are tender, rotating 1/2 turn at half done. Yield: 4 servings.

COOKING

Place foil packets on hot coals or a campfire grill for 30 to 40 minutes.

Or place foil packets in covered grill on medium-low heat for 18 to 22 minutes.

Lemon Barbecued Chicken

3 chicken breasts, bone-in
3 tablespoons onion, chopped
3 tablespoons butter
3 tablespoons brown sugar
3/4 teaspoon dry mustard
3/4 teaspoon salt
3/4 teaspoon pepper
3 tablespoons lemon juice
Heavy duty aluminum foil – 3 pieces of 18" x 24"

Spray foil with non-stick cooking spray. Lightly brown chicken in butter. Center one piece of chicken on each piece of foil. In the same skillet, sauté the onions; sprinkle over chicken.

Mix together brown sugar, mustard, salt and pepper. Sprinkle 1/3 of the brown sugar mixture on top of each chicken breast. Rinse skillet with 3 tablespoons lemon juice and pour over chicken.

Fold the foil tightly to form a flat packet, crimping seams securely. Cook using one of the options below. Yield: 3 servings.

COOKING

Place foil packet on hot coals or a campfire grill for 30 to 45 minutes.

Or place foil packet in covered grill on medium-low heat for 22 to 25 minutes.

Italian-Style Chicken

1 2 1/2 to 3 lb. chicken, cut up, bone-in
4 small potatoes
2 medium zucchini
1/4 cup sliced pitted ripe olives
1 can tomato sauce, 8 oz.
2 teaspoons dried oregano, crushed
2 tablespoons butter or margarine
Parmesan cheese, shredded
Salt and pepper to taste
Heavy duty aluminum foil – 4 pieces 18" x 18"

Spray foil with non-stick cooking spray. Cut potatoes into 1/8-inch slices; divide onto 4 pieces of foil; sprinkle with salt and pepper. Cut zucchini into 1/4-inch slices; place on top of potatoes. Top with chicken pieces, olives, tomato sauce, oregano, and more salt and pepper. Dot with butter or margarine.

Fold the foil loosely to form a tent packet, folding and crimping seams tightly. Cook using one of the options below. Add parmesan cheese to the top of ingredients in packet when done. Yield: 4 servings.

COOKING

Place foil packet on hot coals or a campfire grill for 45 to 60 minutes, turning occasionally.

Or place foil packet in covered grill on medium-low heat for 30 to 35 minutes, turning occasionally.

Chicken with Mushrooms

2 chicken breasts, split in half, bone-in
4 tablespoons butter
1/2 lb. fresh mushrooms, sliced or 1 can, 6 oz., drained
1/2 teaspoon rosemary
3/4 teaspoon salt
1/4 teaspoon pepper
4 tablespoons flour
1 pint light cream
Heavy duty aluminum foil – 4 pieces of 18" x 24"

In a skillet, brown chicken breasts very lightly in the butter. Spray foil with non-stick cooking spray. Place a chicken breast in center of each piece of foil.

Sauté mushrooms quickly in same skillet and add 1/4 of mixture to each piece of foil; season with rosemary, 1/4 teaspoon salt, 1/4 teaspoon pepper. Add flour to butter remaining in skillet; stir and cook 2 minutes. Add cream, stir and cook until sauce is thickened. Add 1/2 teaspoon salt and a sprinkling of pepper. Pour over chicken breasts, dividing equally.

Fold the foil loosely to form a tent packet, folding and crimping seams tightly. Cook per instructions below. Yield: 4 servings.

COOKING

Place foil packet on hot coals or a campfire grill for 30 to 45 minutes.

Or place foil packet in covered grill on medium-low heat for 22 to 25 minutes.

Ranch Chicken Pouches

4 chicken breasts, boneless and skinless
2 large potatoes
1 onion, chopped
1 green pepper, chopped
3 carrots, chopped
2 celery stalks, chopped
4 tablespoons Ranch dressing
Heavy duty aluminum foil – 4 pieces of 18" x 24"

Boil potatoes for 10 minutes. While potatoes are boiling, chop all ingredients for packets. Cut chicken into bite-size cubes. Drain water from potatoes and cut them into 3/4" cubes.

Spray each piece of foil with non-stick cooking spray. Place a chicken breast in the center of each section of foil. Add 1/4 of each of the rest of the ingredients on top of the chicken. Pour one tablespoon of Ranch dressing over ingredients on each packet.

     Fold the foil loosely to form a tent packet, folding and crimping seams tightly. Yield: 4 servings.

COOKING

Place foil packet on hot coals or a campfire grill for 30 to 40 minutes.

Or place foil packet in covered grill on medium-low heat for 20 to 22 minutes.

Chicken Salad on a Bun

2 cups chicken, chopped
6 green olives, chopped
2 tablespoons pickle relish
1/2 cup mayonnaise
2 hard-boiled eggs, chopped
2 tablespoons onion, chopped
1/4 pound American cheese, cubed in small pieces
12 small hamburger buns
Heavy duty aluminum foil – 12 pieces 18" x 12"

Mix all ingredients together. Divide the chicken mixture evenly between 12 buns.

Wrap each bun in foil, crimping seams tightly. Yield: 6 servings.

COOKING

Place foil packet on hot coals or a campfire grill for 15 to 20 minutes.

Or place foil packet in covered grill on medium-low heat for 7 to 10 minutes.

Chicken & Stuffing

6 small chicken breast halves, boneless, skinless
1 can condensed cream of mushroom soup, 10 3/4 oz.
1 3/4 cups water, divided
1 package chicken stuffing mix, 6 oz.
4 slices ham, sliced thin
1 1/2 cups fresh mushrooms, sliced
1 1/2 cups frozen peas
Heavy duty aluminum foil – 6 pieces of 18" x 24"

Combine soup and 1/4 cup of the water; set aside. Spray each piece of foil with non-stick cooking spray. Combine stuffing mix and 1 1/2 cups water; place stuffing mixture in even amounts in the center of each piece of foil. Place one chicken breast on top of the dressing on each foil sheet. Cover evenly with ham, mushrooms, peas, and soup mixture.

Fold the foil loosely to form a tent packet, folding and crimping seams tightly. Yield: 6 servings.

COOKING

Place foil packet on hot coals or a campfire grill for 30 to 40 minutes.

Or place foil packet in covered grill on medium-low heat for 18 to 22 minutes.

Rotisserie Chicken with Asparagus

1 rotisserie chicken, 2 lbs.
1 bunch asparagus, cut in 1" pieces
1 can sliced mushrooms, drained
1 can Progresso Creamy Tomato Basil soup
Salt and pepper to taste
Heavy duty aluminum foil – 4 pieces of 18" x 24"

Spray foil with non-stick cooking spray. Shred the chicken and place even portions in the center of each piece of foil. Place even portions of asparagus and mushrooms on top of chicken. Spoon 4 tablespoons of the tomato soup on top. Season with salt and pepper.

Fold packets up loosely to form a tent packet, folding and crimping seams tightly. Cook over medium heat until good and hot.

COOKING

Place foil packet on hot coals or a campfire grill for 15 minutes.

Or place foil packet in uncovered grill on medium-low heat for 15 minutes.

Chicken Camping Meal

1 lb. chicken breast, boneless and skinless
1 red bell pepper, sliced into strips
1 yellow bell pepper, sliced into strips
1 package fresh sliced mushrooms, 8 oz.
1 medium onion, diced large
4 garlic cloves, sliced
4 small potatoes, diced
Juice of one lemon
1/4 cup olive oil
Heavy duty aluminum foil – 4 sheets 18" x 24"
Large Ziploc bag

Cut each chicken breast into cubes. Place all the ingredients into a Ziploc bag and mix well. Spray foil with non-stick cooking spray. Place even portions of the chicken mixture on the center of each foil square.

Fold the foil loosely to form a tent packet, folding and crimping seams tightly. Chicken should be opaque in color and potatoes should be tender when done. Yield: 4 servings.

COOKING

Place foil packet on hot coals or a campfire grill for 30 to 40 minutes.

Or place foil packet in covered grill on medium-low heat for 18 to 22 minutes.

Chicken Italian

4 chicken breasts, boneless and skinless
1 small onion, sliced
4 Roma tomatoes
1 green or yellow bell pepper
1/2 cup Italian dressing
Heavy duty aluminum foil – 4 pieces 18" x 20"

Cut each tomato in half. Spray foil with non-stick cooking spray. Cut the bell pepper into wedges. In the center of each foil, place a chicken breast. Then divide the onion slices, bell pepper and tomatoes evenly between the 4 pieces of foil, layered on top of the chicken. Pour 2 tablespoons of dressing on top of the ingredients in each packet.

Fold the foil loosely to form a tent packet, folding and crimping seams tightly. Cook as instructed below, rotating packets 1/2 turn after 10 minutes.

COOKING

Place foil packet on hot coals or a campfire grill for 30 to 40 minutes.

Or place foil packet in covered grill on medium-low heat for 18 to 22 minutes.

Grilled Chicken Dinner

2 chicken breasts, bone-in
2 medium potatoes
2 large carrots, cut into pieces
1 cup yellow or zucchini squash
2 tablespoons onion soup mix
1 can condensed cream of chicken soup, diluted with 1/2 cup of water
Heavy duty aluminum foil – 2 pieces 18" x 24"

Peel the potatoes and cut into quarters. Cut the carrots and squash in half lengthwise, then into 1 to 2 inch chunks. Spray foil with non-stick cooking spray. Place a chicken breast in center of each piece of foil. Place vegetables around chicken. Sprinkle with onion soup mix. Top with chicken soup.

Fold foil loosely to form a tent packet, folding and crimping seams tightly. Grill uncovered until tender. Yield: 2 servings.

COOKING

Place foil packet on hot coals or a campfire grill for 45 to 60 minutes.

Or place foil packet in covered grill on medium-low heat for 30 to 35 minutes.

Campfire Fajitas

1 lb. chicken breast, boneless and skinless
1 bell pepper, cut into thin slices
1 onion, chopped
4 or 8 flour tortillas
1 package fajita seasoning
1/4 cup water
Heavy duty aluminum foil – 4 pieces 18" x 18"

Toppings:
1 cup Colby jack cheese, shredded
Chunky salsa
Sour cream

Wrap the tortillas in foil and place near the campfire to heat slowly. Slice the chicken breasts into thin slices. Combine the fajita seasoning and water, then add the chicken, onion and pepper and mix well.

Spray foil with non-stick cooking spray and place equal portions of the fajita mixture on each foil square.

Fold the foil tightly to form a flat packet, crimping seams securely. Packets should not be placed directly in fire. To serve, place fajita mixture on a flour tortilla and add your favorite toppings.

COOKING

Place foil packet on hot coals or a campfire grill for 30 to 40 minutes.

Or place foil packet in covered grill on medium-low heat for 18 to 20 minutes.

Spanish Chicken

3 chicken breasts, bone-in
2 tablespoons olive oil
6 small white onions
1 green pepper, chopped in large pieces
1 teaspoon garlic powder
1 teaspoon salt
1/2 teaspoon pepper
1 can tomato sauce, 8 oz.
Heavy duty aluminum foil – 3 pieces of 18" x 24"

Spray foil with non-stick cooking spray. Brown chicken in olive oil, then place each breast on a piece of foil.

On top of each chicken, add 2 small white onions and 1/3 of the green pepper. Season with garlic powder, salt and pepper. Spoon the tomato sauce over the chicken, dividing it equally.

Fold the foil tightly to form a flat packet, crimping seams securely. Cook using one of the options below. Yield: 3 servings.

COOKING

Place foil packet on hot coals or a campfire grill for 30 to 45 minutes.

Or place foil packet in covered grill on medium-low heat for 22 to 25 minutes.

Barbecued Chicken in Foil

1 1/2 lbs. chicken pieces, cut up, bone-in
3 tablespoons ketchup
2 tablespoons vinegar
1 tablespoon lemon juice
2 tablespoons Worcestershire sauce
1/4 cup water
2 tablespoons butter, melted
2 teaspoons salt
1 teaspoon dry mustard
2 teaspoons chili powder
1 teaspoon paprika
1/4 teaspoon red pepper
Heavy duty aluminum foil – 2 pieces 18" x 24"

In a bowl, combine all ingredients except chicken. Dip the cut-up chicken in the sauce and arrange in a single layer, half on each foil. Spoon remaining sauce over top of chicken.

Fold the foil tightly to form a flat packet, crimping seams tightly. Cook using one of the options below or until the chicken is tender.

COOKING

Place foil packet on hot coals or a campfire grill for 30 to 45 minutes.

Or place foil packet in covered grill on medium-low heat for 22 to 25 minutes.

Butter Baked Chicken

4 chicken breasts with wings, bone-in
1/4 cup margarine
Salt and pepper to taste
Heavy duty aluminum foil – 4 pieces 18" x 24"

Remove the skin from the chicken. Sprinkle salt and pepper on chicken. Turn the rib side up and put two squares of butter on each piece. Spray foil with non-stick cooking spray. Wrap each piece of chicken in foil, rib sides up,

 Fold the foil tightly to form flat packets with tightly crimped seams.

COOKING

Place foil packet on hot coals or a campfire grill for 30 to 45 minutes.

Or place foil packet in covered grill on medium-low heat for 22 to 25 minutes.

FISH
FOIL
PACKETS

Fish

Teriyaki Fish in Foil

2 lbs. halibut
1 can pineapple slices, 20 oz.
1/4 cup soy sauce
1 tablespoon brown sugar
2 tablespoons vegetable oil
1 teaspoon flour
1/2 cup dry white wine
1/2 teaspoon dry mustard
Heavy duty aluminum foil – 6 pieces 18" x 24"

Combine soy sauce, brown sugar, oil, flour, wine and mustard in small saucepan. Bring to boil, reduce heat and simmer for 3 minutes. Cool.

Brush 6 slices of pineapple with the soy sauce mixture, reserve a few tablespoons of the mixture for serving and marinate fish for 15 minutes in the remainder of the soy sauce mixture. Discard the soy sauce mixture used to marinate the fish.

Spray foil with non-stick cooking spray. Place the fish in the middle of the foil and add the pineapple on top.

Fold the foil loosely to form a tent packet, folding and crimping seams tightly. Cook as instructed below or until fish flakes easily with fork. Remove to warm platter and spoon any remaining sauce onto fish and fruit. Yield: Serves 6.

COOKING

Place foil packet on hot coals or an uncovered hot grill for 10 to 15 minutes for fish one inch thick. Add 5 to 7 minutes per 1/2" of thickness. Rotate packet 1/2 turn halfway through cooking. Cook until fish flakes easily with a fork.

Italian Fish Packets

2 halibut fillets
1 cup diced tomatoes, canned or fresh
8 black olives
2 teaspoons capers
1 tablespoon extra-virgin olive oil
2 teaspoons chopped garlic
1/4 teaspoon dried thyme
1/8 teaspoon dried rosemary
Heavy duty aluminum foil – 2 pieces 18" x 12"

Spray the foil with non-stick cooking spray. Place a fish fillet in the center of each piece of foil. On top of each fish, add half of the tomatoes, olives and capers. Mix the garlic, thyme and rosemary together. Sprinkle half on top of each fish. Drizzle each with olive oil.

        Fold the foil tightly to form a flat packet, crimping seams tightly. Cook as directed below, until fish is opaque throughout and flakes easily with fork. Yield: 2 servings.

COOKING

Place foil packets on hot coals or an uncovered medium hot grill for 10 to 12 minutes.

Salmon Supreme

2 salmon filets, skin attached
1 red onion, sliced thinly
1 red bell pepper, sliced
8 ounces fresh mushrooms, sliced
4 tablespoons butter
Heavy duty aluminum foil – 2 pieces 18" x 20"

In a skillet, sauté sliced vegetables in butter until slightly soft. Spray foil with non-stick cooking spray. Put each piece of salmon, skin side down, in the center of a piece of foil. Top with vegetable mixture.

Fold the foil loosely to form a tent packet, folding and crimping seams tightly. Place on a preheated grill and cook using one of the options below. Salmon should flake easily with fork when done. Yield: 2 servings.

COOKING

Place foil packet on hot coals or an uncovered hot grill for 10 to 15 minutes for fish one inch thick. Add 5 to 7 minutes per 1/2" of thickness. Rotate packet 1/2 turn halfway through cooking.

Coconut Shrimp

2 lb. large shrimp, peeled
4 scallions, chopped
2/3 cup coconut milk
4 tablespoons lime juice
Heavy duty aluminum foil – 2 pieces 18" x 24"

Combine the scallions, coconut milk and lime juice. Add the shrimp and mix well. Spray the foil with non-stick cooking spray. Place half of the shrimp mixture on each foil in a single layer.

Fold the foil tightly to form a flat packet, crimping seams tightly. Cook using one of the options below. Turn the flat packet over halfway through cooking. Check shrimp after 10 minutes for doneness. Yield: 4 servings.

COOKING

Place foil packet on hot coals or a campfire grill for 15 to 20 minutes.

Or place foil packet in covered grill on medium-low heat for 10 to 15 minutes.

Easy Spanish Fillets

4 tilapia fillets
2 cups fresh salsa
24 black olives
2 teaspoons lime juice
Heavy duty aluminum foil – 4 pieces 18" x 12"

Spray the foil with non-stick cooking spray. Place a fish fillet in the center of each piece of foil. On top of each fish, add 1/2 cup salsa, 6 black olives and 1/2 teaspoon lime juice.

Fold the foil tightly to form a flat packet, crimping seams tightly. Cook as directed below, until fish is opaque throughout and flakes easily with fork. Yield: 4 servings.

COOKING

Place foil packet on hot coals or an uncovered hot grill for 10 to 15 minutes for fish one inch thick or less. Add 5 to 7 minutes per 1/2" of thickness. Rotate packet 1/2 turn halfway through cooking.

Fish with Spinach

4 fish fillets
1 onion
1 package baby spinach leaves, 9 oz. bag
4 Tesoro or plum tomatoes, chopped
1 tablespoon garlic powder
Salt and pepper to taste
4 tablespoons olive oil
2 tablespoons balsamic vinegar
Heavy duty aluminum foil – 4 pieces 18" x 20"

Spray the foil with non-stick cooking spray. Rinse and pat the fish dry. Place a fish fillet in the center of each foil. Cut the onion into 8 pieces. Add 2 pieces of onion to each foil with the fish.

In a bowl, mix the spinach leaves and tomatoes. Sprinkle with garlic powder, salt and pepper, olive oil and vinegar. Mix well. Place 1/4 of the spinach mixture on top of each fish.

Fold the foil loosely to form a tent packet, folding and crimping seams tightly. Cook with one of the options below until fish flakes easily with fork. Yield: 4 servings.

COOKING

Place foil packet on hot coals or a campfire grill for 25 to 40 minutes.

Or place foil packet in covered grill on medium-low heat for 18 to 22 minutes.

Healthy Grilled Salmon

1 1/2 lbs. salmon fillets
2 tablespoons extra virgin olive oil
Salt and pepper to taste
1 medium lemon, cut into 12 slices
Heavy duty aluminum foil – 4 pieces 18" x 18"

Skin salmon and cut into four sections. Spray foil with non-stick cooking spray. Place a salmon section on the center of each foil. Brush both sides of salmon with olive oil. Sprinkle salt and pepper over salmon. Top each fish with three lemon slices overlapping each other.

Fold the foil tightly to form a flat packet, crimping seams securely. Place on a preheated grill and cook as directed below. Yield: 4 servings.

COOKING

Place foil packet on hot coals or an uncovered hot grill for 10 to 15 minutes for fish one inch thick. Add 5 to 7 minutes per 1/2" of thickness. Turn the flat packet over halfway through cooking. Salmon should flake easily with fork when done.

Fresh Perch Fillets

6 fresh perch fillets
1/4 cup butter
1/2 cup onion, chopped
1/4 cup parsley, snipped
2 stalks celery, sliced
1/2 lb. fresh mushrooms, sliced
1/4 teaspoon salt
Freshly ground pepper
3 tomatoes, cut in half
Heavy duty aluminum foil – 6 pieces 18" x 20"

Melt butter in skillet; add onion, parsley and celery. Cook until crisp-tender. Add mushrooms, cook 5 minutes; season with salt and pepper. Spray foil with non-stick cooking spray. Arrange a fish fillet on each piece of foil. Divide vegetables evenly over fish. Top each with a tomato half.

Fold the foil loosely to form tent packets, folding and crimping seams tightly. Cook using one of the options below. Yield: 3 to 6 servings.

COOKING

Place foil packet on hot coals or an uncovered hot grill for 10 to 15 minutes for fish one inch thick. Add 5 to 7 minutes per 1/2" of thickness. Rotate packet 1/2 turn halfway through cooking. Cook until fish flakes easily with a fork and vegetables are done.

Salmon in Sauce

1 1/2 lbs. salmon fillets
1 tablespoon olive oil
1/2 teaspoon dried dill
1/4 teaspoon pepper

Dill Sauce:
1 cup chicken broth
1 tablespoon spicy brown mustard
1 tablespoon cornstarch
3/4 cup evaporated milk
2 teaspoons lemon juice
1/2 cup fresh dill, chopped
Heavy duty aluminum foil – 4 pieces 18" x 24"

Cut salmon fillet into 4 pieces. Spray foil with non-stick cooking spray. Place salmon in the center of the foil. Brush both sides with olive oil. Sprinkle with pepper and dried dill.

Fold the foil tightly to form a flat packet, crimping seams securely. Cook using one of the options below.

Dill Sauce - Combine broth, mustard, cornstarch and milk in a bowl. Add lemon juice and fresh dill and mix well. Cook in a small saucepan, stirring constantly, over medium heat until thickened. Place salmon on serving plate and pour sauce on top. Yield: 4 servings.

COOKING

Place foil packet on hot coals or an uncovered hot grill for 10 to 15 minutes for fish one inch thick. Add 5 to 7 minutes per 1/2" of thickness. Turn the flat packet over halfway through cooking. Cook until fish flakes easily with a fork.

Oriental Fish Packets

2 cups cooked rice
1 lb. fish fillets
12 scallops
12 shrimp, peeled, deveined
1/2 cup shredded carrot
1/2 cup sliced red bell pepper
1/2 cup sliced mushrooms
1/2 cup baby corn
1/2 cup snow peas
1/4 cup orange juice
1/4 cup soy sauce
1 large garlic clove, finely sliced
2 teaspoons grated ginger root
Pinch of red pepper flakes (optional)
Heavy duty aluminum foil – 4 pieces 18" x 24"

Spray each piece of foil with non-stick cooking spray. Spoon 1/2 cup rice in the center of each piece of foil. Rinse the fish and pat dry. Arrange the fish, scallops and shrimp over the rice, dividing evenly among the 4 pieces of foil. Top each portion with 1/4 of the carrots, 1/4 of the bell peppers, 1/4 of the mushrooms, 1/4 of the baby corn and 1/4 of the snow peas.

Whisk the orange juice, soy sauce, garlic, ginger root and red pepper flakes together in a small bowl. Drizzle the orange juice mixture evenly over the 4 sets of fish and vegetables.

Fold the foil loosely to form a tent packet, folding and crimping seams tightly. Cook as instructed below until the fish flakes easily with a fork and the vegetables are tender. Yield: 4 servings.

COOKING

Place foil packet on hot coals or an uncovered hot grill for 10 to 15 minutes for fish one inch thick. Add 5 to 7 minutes per 1/2" of thickness. Rotate packet 1/2 turn halfway through cooking.

63

Sea Bass and Veggies

1 lb. sea bass, cut into 4 portions (you can leave skin on)
2 cups carrots, cut in julienne strips
1 small leek, cut in julienne strips
2 cups frozen corn
1/2 cup tomatoes, sliced
2 teaspoons fresh basil, coarsely chopped
4 teaspoons lemon juice
1 teaspoon minced fresh ginger (or 1/2 teaspoon dry)
1/4 teaspoon black pepper
1/8 teaspoon salt
Heavy duty aluminum foil – 4 pieces 18" x 20"

Spray foil with non-stick cooking spray. Arrange 1/4 of carrots, leeks, corn and tomatoes and basil in center of piece of foil; top with fish. Sprinkle fish with lemon juice, ginger, pepper and salt.

Fold the foil loosely to form a tent packet, folding and crimping seams tightly. Cook as instructed below until fish flakes easily with fork and veggies are tender-crisp. Yield: 4 servings.

COOKING

Place foil packet on hot coals or an uncovered hot grill for 10 to 15 minutes for fish one inch thick. Add 5 to 7 minutes per 1/2" of thickness. Rotate packet 1/2 turn halfway through cooking.

Wrapped Shrimp

6 oz. shrimp, cleaned and deveined
1 cup French-style string beans
2 stalks of celery
1 tablespoon tomato juice
1 tablespoon dehydrated onion flakes
1/2 teaspoon salt
1/4 teaspoon minced garlic
Heavy duty aluminum foil – 18" x 24"

Cut the celery into 8 thin slices. Spray foil with non-stick cooking spray. Place the beans in the middle of the foil with the celery; add shrimp on top of beans. Sprinkle the remaining ingredients on top.

Fold the foil loosely to form a tent packet, folding and crimping seams tightly. Cook using one of the options below. Yield: 2 servings.

COOKING

Place foil packet on hot coals or an uncovered hot grill for 7 to 10 minutes. Rotate packet 1/2 turn halfway through cooking.

Grilled Tilapia

2 tilapia fillets
2 garlic cloves
1/4 teaspoon salt
1/4 teaspoon black pepper
2 slices of lemon
2 ice cubes
Heavy duty aluminum foil – 2 pieces 18" x 20"

Spray foil with non-stick cooking spray. Place a slice of lemon on each foil. Cut the garlic cloves in half and rub on both sides of the tilapia, then place garlic clove on foil pieces. Put the tilapia fillet on top of lemon and garlic on the foil, sprinkle with pepper and salt.

Put the ice cube on the fillet and fold the foil loosely to form a tent packet, folding and crimping seams tightly. Cook using one of the options below. Yield: Serves 2.

COOKING

Place foil packet on hot coals or a medium hot uncovered grill for 10 to 15 minutes for fish one inch thick. Add 5 to 7 minutes per 1/2" of thickness. Rotate packet 1/2 turn halfway through cooking. Cook until fish flakes easily with a fork.

Fish Fillets in Foil

4 fillets of fish (red snapper, redfish or catfish)
1 cup fresh tomato salsa
Hot cooked white rice
Lime wedges as garnish
Heavy duty aluminum foil – 4 pieces 18" x 20"

Spray foil with non-stick cooking spray. Place a fish fillet on each foil. Top with 1/4 cup salsa.

 Fold the foil tightly to form a flat packet, crimping seams securely.

Cook as instructed below until fish flakes easily with fork. Serve each fillet with its sauce on cooked rice and garnish with lime wedges. Yield: 4 servings.

COOKING

Place foil packet on hot coals or an uncovered hot grill for 10 to 15 minutes for fish one inch thick. Add 5 to 7 minutes per 1/2" of thickness. Turn the flat packet over halfway through cooking.

Savory Fillets

2 lbs. fish fillets
Salt and pepper to taste
2 tablespoons lemon juice
2 tablespoons margarine
1 teaspoon oregano
Heavy duty aluminum foil – 4 pieces 18" x 20"

Divide fish into 4 portions and place in the center of each piece of foil. Sprinkle with salt and pepper. Add 1/2 tablespoon lemon juice to each foil; dot with margarine. Sprinkle each with oregano.

Fold the foil tightly to form a flat packet, crimping seams tightly. Cook as below until fish flakes easily with fork. Turn the flat packet over halfway through cooking. Yield: 4 servings.

COOKING

Place foil packet on hot coals or a campfire grill for 20 to 35 minutes.

Or place foil packet in covered grill on medium-low heat for 15 to 20 minutes.

Quick and Easy Fish

2 or 3 shallots, finely chopped
2 tablespoons fresh parsley, finely diced
1/2 cup butter
1/4 teaspoon lemon juice
Heavy duty aluminum foil – 18" x 24"

Melt the butter in a saucepan over low to medium heat. Add shallots, parsley and lemon juice. Cook over low heat until the shallots are transparent and the mixture is reduced to a thin paste.

Use any or all of these items:

1 pound any fillets (salmon, haddock, sole)
1 pound scallops
1 pound shelled shrimp

Spray foil with non-stick cooking spray. Place the fish, etc. on the foil. Top with the shallots mixture.

    Fold the foil loosely to form a tent packet, folding and crimping seams tightly. Cook using one of the options below.

COOKING

Place foil packet on hot coals or an uncovered hot grill for 10 to 15 minutes for fish one inch thick. Add 5 to 7 minutes per 1/2" of thickness. Rotate packet 1/2 turn halfway through cooking. Cook until fish flakes easily with a fork.

Shrimp Scampi in Foil

2 lbs. shrimp, fresh or frozen, with shell
1 small clove garlic, finely minced
1 cup butter, melted
1/4 teaspoon rosemary
1/4 teaspoon basil
3 tablespoons lemon juice
1/2 teaspoon salt
1/4 teaspoon pepper
Heavy duty aluminum foil – 6 pieces 18" x 8"

If shrimp are frozen with shell, thaw just to separate. Rinse in cold water, drain and place in boiling water. Bring to a boil and cook 1 minute. Drain; cool just enough to handle. Remove shells and dark vein. If frozen shrimp are already shelled and cleaned, use only 1 pound and thaw until they can be separated.

Melt butter in a saucepan. Mince garlic; add to butter along with rosemary and basil. Cook on low heat for a few minutes to frizzle the garlic.

Add lemon juice. Arrange 10 shrimp to a serving on squares of heavy duty foil. Pour butter mixture over shrimp; sprinkle each serving with salt and pepper.

Bring foil up over shrimp, and twist ends together at top to seal. Yield: 6 servings.

COOKING

Place foil packets on hot coals or an uncovered medium hot grill for 10 to 12 minutes or until thoroughly cooked, depending on size of shrimp.

Perch and Vegetable Packets

1 lb. frozen perch (or other lean fish)
1 package frozen broccoli, 16 oz.
1 package baby carrots, 8 oz.
1 teaspoon dried dill weed
1/2 teaspoon salt
1/4 teaspoon pepper
4 tablespoons dry white wine (or apple juice)
Heavy duty aluminum foil – 4 pieces 18" x 20"

Divide fish into 4 portions and place in the center of each piece of foil. Top each with 1/2 of the broccoli and carrots. Sprinkle with dill weed, salt and pepper. Pour 1 tablespoon wine over each set of vegetables.

Fold the foil loosely to form a tent packet, folding and crimping seams tightly. Cook as instructed below or until fish flakes easily with fork. Yield: Serves 4.

COOKING

Place foil packet on hot coals or an uncovered hot grill for 10 to 15 minutes for fish one inch thick. Add 5 to 7 minutes per 1/2" of thickness. Rotate packet 1/2 turn halfway through cooking. Cook until fish flakes easily with a fork and vegetables are done.

Tuna Sandwich Filling

1 can tuna (5 oz.)
1 cup celery, finely chopped
1/2 cup shredded American cheese
1/4 cup mayonnaise
1 tablespoon onion, grated
3 small hamburger buns
Heavy duty aluminum foil – 3 pieces 18" x 18"

Combine all ingredients. Spread tuna mixture on buns and wrap securely in foil.

Fold the foil tightly to form a flat packet, crimping seams tightly. Turn packets 1/2 turn halfway through cooking.

COOKING

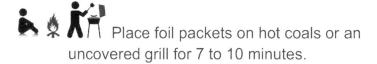 Place foil packets on hot coals or an uncovered grill for 7 to 10 minutes.

BEEF
FOIL
PACKETS

Beef

Supper on French Bread

1 loaf French bread
1 1/4 lbs. lean ground beef
2/3 cup evaporated milk (5 oz. can)
1/2 cup cracker crumbs
1 egg
1/2 cup onion, chopped
1 tablespoon prepared mustard
1 teaspoon salt
1/8 teaspoon pepper
2 cups shredded American cheese
Heavy duty aluminum foil - 2 pieces 18" x 24"

Brown the ground beef and drain. Cut bread loaf in half lengthwise. Combine beef and remaining ingredients; spread mixture over top surface of each half loaf. Spray foil with non-stick cooking spray.

Wrap each half loaf in foil, crimping seams tightly. To serve, cut into slices. Yield: 6 to 8 servings.

COOKING

Place foil packet on hot coals or a campfire grill for 15 to 25 minutes.

Or place foil packet in uncovered grill on medium-low heat for 15 minutes.

Campfire Meatball Sandwiches

Precooking the meatballs at home and freezing them saves time when making these camping packets. Or purchase premade frozen meatballs to save even more time.

12 frozen and or pre-cooked homemade meatballs
4 hoagie rolls or submarine buns
Jar of pizza sauce
6 ounces shredded Monterey Jack cheese or mozzarella cheese
Heavy duty aluminum foil – 4 pieces 18" x 18"

Warm the meat balls, if possible. Slice the top of each roll being careful not to cut all the way through. Remove enough of the bread from the bottom half of the rolls to make a shell.

Spread pizza sauce on the cut top and bottom of each roll. Add 3 meatballs to each roll. (Cut meatballs in half if necessary) Add shredded cheese on top of the meatballs and close the sandwich. Be sure the cheese stays inside the bun.

Wrap each sandwich securely in foil. Cook until meat is hot and cheese is melted. Yield: 4 servings.

Meatballs to make at home:

1 lb. ground round
3/4 cup bread crumbs
1/2 teaspoon garlic powder
1 tablespoon parsley
2 teaspoons Italian seasoning
1 egg, well beaten

In a bowl, mix all ingredients. Form into 12 meatballs. Place meatballs in a baking dish and bake at 350 degrees F. for 15 to 20 minutes or until cooked through. Remove with a slotted spoon to paper towels to drain.

COOKING

Place foil packet on hot coals or a campfire grill for 7 to 10 minutes.

Or place foil packet in covered grill on medium-low heat for 5 to 7 minutes.

Corned Beef on Buns

1 can corned beef, 7 oz.
1 cup sharp Cheddar cheese, shredded
2 tablespoons pickle relish
1/4 cup onion
2 tablespoons Worcestershire sauce
1/2 cup black olives, chopped
1/2 cup ketchup
4 hamburger buns
Heavy duty aluminum foil – 4 pieces 18" x 18"

Mix all ingredients together. Fill hamburger buns with mixture.

Wrap each burger in foil separately. Cook using one of the options below.

COOKING

Place foil packet on hot coals or a campfire grill for 10 minutes.

Or place foil packet in uncovered grill on medium-low heat for 10 minutes.

Foil Steak Supper

1 1/2 lbs. chuck steak, 1 inch thick
1 envelope onion soup mix
3 medium carrots, quartered
2 stalks celery, cut into sticks
3 medium potatoes, halved
2 tablespoons margarine
1/2 teaspoon salt
Heavy duty aluminum foil – 18" x 30"

Spray foil with non-stick cooking spray. Place meat in center of foil and sprinkle with onion soup mix. Cover with vegetables. Dot with butter; sprinkle with salt.

Fold foil loosely to form a tent packet, folding and sealing seams tightly to hold in juices. Cook using one of the options below. Yield: Serves 4.

COOKING

Place foil packet on hot coals or a campfire grill for about 45 minutes or until done.

Or place foil packet in covered grill on medium-low heat for about 30 minutes or until done.

Pizzaburgers in Foil

1 1/2 lbs. hamburger
1 medium onion, chopped
1 can tomato sauce, 8 oz.
1/2 teaspoon garlic powder
Salt and pepper to taste
Shredded mozzarella cheese, 8 oz.
8 chopped green olives
1 teaspoon oregano
6 hamburger buns
Heavy duty aluminum foil – 6 pieces – 18" x 18"

Brown the hamburger and onion. Drain. Let cool. When cool, mix in tomato sauce, garlic powder, salt and pepper. Add the mozzarella cheese and chopped olives. Spoon on hamburger buns. Sprinkle lightly with oregano.

Wrap each bun separately in foil. Seal packets well.

COOKING

Place foil packet on hot coals or a campfire grill for 10 to 15 minutes per side.

Or place foil packet in covered grill on medium-low heat for 5 to 7 minutes per side.

Hobo Dinners

1 lb. hamburger
1 onion, sliced
1 can of corn (or package of frozen corn)
4 medium potatoes, cubed
Salt and pepper
Heavy duty aluminum foil – 4 pieces 18" x 20"

Spray foil lightly with non-stick cooking spray. Place 1/4 of the hamburger in the center of each foil. (Note: hamburger can be browned first, if desired) Add the sliced onions on top of the hamburger. Salt and pepper the hamburger. Add corn on top, then the cubed potatoes.

Fold the foil loosely to form a tent packet, folding and crimping seams tightly. Yield: 4 servings.

COOKING

Place foil packet on hot coals or a campfire grill for 20 to 40 minutes.

Or place foil packet in covered grill on medium-low heat for 18 to 22 minutes.

Corned Beef Brisket

1 corned beef brisket, vacuum packaged (2 - 3 lbs.)
1 onion, sliced
1 small orange, sliced
Heavy duty aluminum foil - 18" x 24"

Preheat grill. Unwrap the brisket and rinse it off well to remove any surface brining liquid or salt. Blot dry with paper towels. Sear the brisket on the grill, high heat, for about 8 minutes, turning once. Remove brisket from grill and put in the center of the foil; surround with onion and orange slices.

Bring edges of foil together and seal with double fold around brisket to form airtight package. Grill on low heat turning one-half turn every 30 minutes. Grill until the internal temperature of the meat has reached 160 to 165 degrees F for medium. Yield: 6 servings.

COOKING

Place foil packet on hot coals or a campfire grill for 1 1/2 to 2 1/2 hours.

Or place foil packet in uncovered grill on low heat for 1 to 2 hours.

Grilled Chuck Roast

3 to 3-1/2 lbs. chuck roast - cut rather thick
Adolph's meat tenderizer
4 teaspoons corn oil or canola oil
2 teaspoons Kitchen Bouquet
1 onion, sliced
Heavy duty aluminum foil – 18" x 24"

Trim fat from meat. With a fork, prick meat, then salt well with tenderizer on both sides. Let meat stand for 1 hour in refrigerator. Mix oil and Kitchen Bouquet together and brush mixture over all parts of the meat. Let stand for 1 more hour in refrigerator.

Spray foil with non-stick cooking spray. Place roast in the center of the foil and add sliced onions on top of meat.

Fold the foil tightly to form a flat packet with securely crimped seams.

Cook until meat is thoroughly cooked. Turn foil packet occasionally. Time will vary because of thickness of meat and temperature of fire, about 1/2 hour on each side. Grill until the internal temperature of the meat has reached 160 to 165 degrees F for medium. Yield: 5 servings.

COOKING

Place foil packet on hot coals or a campfire grill for about 30 to 45 minutes **on each side**.

Or place foil packet in covered grill on medium-low heat for 30 minutes **on each side.**

PORK
FOIL
PACKETS

Pork

Chinese Glazed Ribs

2 lbs. baby back ribs
1 tablespoon liquid smoke
1/2 cup chili sauce
1/4 cup hoisin sauce
1 tablespoon honey
1/4 teaspoon salt
Dash of cayenne pepper
Heavy duty aluminum foil – 18" x 24"

Mix all ingredients together except ribs. Coat each rib with the sauce and put in a single layer on the foil.

Fold the foil tightly to form a flat packet, crimping seams securely. Cook in covered grill, turning occasionally.

COOKING

Place foil packet in covered grill on medium-low heat for 60 minutes.

Ham and Cheese Rolls

Diced, boneless ham, 12 oz. package
1/2 cup cheddar cheese, shredded
1/3 cup green onions, chopped
1/2 cup stuffed green olives, chopped
1/2 cup chili sauce
2 hard-boiled eggs, chopped
3 tablespoons mayonnaise
6 frankfurter buns
Heavy duty aluminum foil – 6 pieces 18" x 18"

Combine all ingredients, except buns, and mix well. Pile mixture into buns.

Wrap each bun separately in foil. Yield: 6 servings.

COOKING

Place foil packet on hot coals or a campfire grill for 15 to 20 minutes.

Or place foil packet in covered grill on medium-low heat for 7 to 10 minutes.

Squash with Pork Chops

4 pork chops, 1 inch thick
1/2 teaspoon salt
1/4 teaspoon pepper
2 acorn squash
4 tablespoons margarine
4 tablespoons brown sugar
4 tablespoons honey
Heavy duty aluminum foil – 4 pieces 18" x 20"

Trim any fat from pork chops. Place one chop in the center of each piece of foil. Salt and pepper each pork chop. Cut each squash in half and remove seeds and fibers. Fill center hole of squash with 1 tablespoon each of margarine, brown sugar and honey. Add a squash, cut side up, on top of each pork chop.

Wrap tightly in foil. Cook using one of the options below until squash and pork chop are cooked through and tender. Yield: 4 servings.

COOKING

Place foil packet on hot coals or a campfire grill for 60 to 75 minutes.

Or place foil packet in covered grill on medium-low heat for 60 minutes.

Grilled Ham & New Potatoes

2 slices well-cured ham, fat trimmed
1/2 cup orange juice
1/2 cup brown sugar
1/2 cup honey
1/2 teaspoon dry mustard
12 small new potatoes
3 tablespoons butter
Salt and pepper to taste
1 tablespoon fresh, chopped parsley
Heavy duty aluminum foil – 18" x 24"

Scrub the new potatoes and cut in halves or quarters, leaving skins on. Arrange in a single layer on foil. Spread with butter, salt, pepper, and parsley.

Fold the foil loosely to form a tent packet, folding and crimping seams tightly. Place on rack over hot, gray coals and grill.

Snip edges of ham so it won't buckle and curl. Place on grill over hot, gray coals. Stir together the orange juice, brown sugar, honey, and mustard. Baste ham slices constantly, turning once. Yield: 4 servings.

COOKING

Place potato foil packet on hot coals or a campfire grill for 20 minutes.

Or place potato foil packet in covered grill on medium-low heat for 10 to 15 minutes.

Campfire Bean Dogs

1 package hot dogs
1 package hot dog buns
Beans as desired
Heavy duty aluminum foil – 18" x 18"

Boston Style:
Split hot dogs lengthwise, spread with sweet pickle relish, and fill with Boston baked beans. Wrap each in foil. Grill on coals, turning once. Toast buns on grill.

Southwest Style:
Split hot dogs lengthwise and fill with chili beans. Wrap each in foil. Grill on coals, turning once. Toast buns on grill.

Arizona Style:
Split hot dogs lengthwise and fill with spicy chili, no beans. Wrap each in foil. Grill on coals, turning once. Toast buns on grill.

Yield: Serves 5.

COOKING

Place foil packet on hot coals or a campfire grill for 10 to 15 minutes.

Or place foil packet in uncovered grill on medium-low heat for about 10 minutes.

Cheesy Sausage Bundles

1 lb. fully cooked beef sausage, cut into 3/4-inch pieces
1/2 cup shredded Cheddar cheese
3/4 cup processed cheese sauce (jar)
1 large sweet onion, sliced
1 large green pepper, sliced into strips
2 medium potatoes, sliced 1/2 inch thick
Heavy duty aluminum foil – 4 pieces 18" x 18"

Spray foil with non-stick cooking spray. In a bowl, combine the cheese and cheese sauce. Add onion, green pepper and potatoes to the cheese mixture and mix.

Place 1/4 of the sausage in the center of each piece of foil. Add 1/4 of the cheese and vegetable mixture to the foil.

 Fold the foil loosely to form a tent packet, folding and crimping seams tightly. Grill until vegetables are tender and meat is hot. Yield: 4 servings.

COOKING

Place foil packet on hot coals or a campfire grill for 35 to 45 minutes.

Or place foil packet in covered grill on medium-low heat for 20 to 25 minutes.

Stuffed Hot Dog Rolls

1 lb. beef hot dogs, cut crosswise into 1/4 inch slices
3/4 lb. sharp Cheddar cheese, cut into 1/2 inch cubes
1/4 cup onion, minced
1/3 cup stuffed green olives, chopped
3 hard-boiled eggs, chopped
1/4 cup chili sauce
1/4 cup mayonnaise
12 hot dog buns
Heavy duty aluminum foil – 12 pieces 18" x 18"

Combine the hot dogs, cheese, onion, olives, eggs, chili sauce and mayonnaise. Open the buns; fill each with about 1/3 cup of hot dog mixture.

Wrap each bun in heavy-duty aluminum foil, twisting the ends. Yield: Makes 12 packets.

COOKING

Place foil packet on hot coals or a campfire grill for 10 to 15 minutes.

Or place foil packet in covered grill on medium-low heat for about 10 minutes.

99

Baby Back Ribs

3 lbs. baby back pork ribs
2 teaspoons garlic powder
1 1/2 teaspoons pepper
1 teaspoon paprika
1 teaspoon brown sugar
1/2 cup water
1 1/2 cups barbecue sauce
Heavy duty aluminum foil - 2 pieces 18" x 24"

Cut each rack of ribs into thirds. On each sheet of foil, place half of the ribs in a single layer. In a bowl, mix the garlic powder, pepper, paprika, and brown sugar. Sprinkle spice mix on the ribs and rub the mixture in, coating evenly.

Make a loose foil packet around the ribs, leaving one end open and sealing seams tightly. Pour 1/4 cup of water through the open end. Fold foil in to seal. Repeat for second packet. Yield: Serves 4.

COOKING

Place foil packet in covered grill on medium-low heat for 45 to 60 minutes. Then carefully remove ribs from foil and place them directly on the grill. Grill for 10 to 15 minutes more in uncovered grill, liberally brushing ribs with barbecue sauce and turning ribs every 5 minutes for even cooking.

Ham and Swiss Sandwiches

1 1/2 lbs. shaved ham
1 package sliced Swiss cheese, 6 oz.
1/2 cup soft butter
2 tablespoons mustard
1 tablespoons grated onion
1 teaspoon poppy seed
12 small hamburger buns
Heavy duty aluminum foil – 12 pieces 18" x 18"

Mix butter, mustard, grated onion and poppy seed. Spread on buns. Add cheese and ham.

Wrap each sandwich securely in foil. Cook until meat is hot and cheese is melted. Yield: 12 servings.

COOKING

Place foil packet on hot coals or a campfire grill for 15 to 20 minutes.

Or place foil packet in covered grill on medium-low heat for 7 to 10 minutes.

Easy Chili Dogs

4 hot dogs
4 hot dog buns
1 can hot dog chili, 15 oz.
1/2 cup onions, chopped
1/2 cup shredded cheddar cheese
Nonstick cooking spray
Heavy duty aluminum foil – 4 pieces 18" x 18"

Lightly spray the foil with cooking spray. Place a hot dog in each hot dog bun. Top each with 3 tablespoons of chili, 2 tablespoons shredded cheese and onion.

Wrap each hot dog separately in the foil and cook until cheese has melted and hot dog is hot.

COOKING

Place foil packet on hot coals or a campfire grill for 10 to 15 minutes.

Or place foil packet in covered grill on medium-low heat for about 10 minutes.

Vegetables

Cheesy Bacon Potatoes

3 large potatoes, sliced
Salt and pepper
4 to 5 slices bacon, cooked and crumbled
1 slice onion
1/2 lb. Velveeta cheese (2 cups cubed)
1/2 cup margarine
Heavy duty aluminum foil – 18" x 24"

Spray the foil with non-stick cooking spray. Place all ingredients on foil in following order: sliced potatoes, salt and pepper, crumbled bacon, onion, cheese and margarine.

 Fold the foil loosely to form a tent packet, folding and crimping seams tightly. Grill, rotating 1/2 turn several times.

COOKING

Place foil packet on hot coals or a campfire grill for 45 minutes to 1 hour.

Or place foil packet in covered grill on medium-low heat for 35 to 45 minutes.

Stuffed Tomatoes

4 tomatoes, cored (reserve cores)
2 tablespoons butter
1 cup cheese garlic croutons, crushed
1 tablespoon butter
2 tablespoons mushrooms, chopped
1/4 cup onion, chopped
1/4 cup green pepper, chopped
1/2 cup shredded cheddar cheese
1 teaspoon pepper
1 teaspoon garlic powder
Heavy duty aluminum foil – 4 pieces 18" x 12"

In a mixing bowl, combine 1/2 cup cored tomato reserve with all remaining ingredients. Spray the foil with non-stick cooking spray.

Spoon mixture into cored tomatoes and wrap in foil. Cook using one of the options below. Yield: 4 servings.

COOKING

Place foil packet on hot coals or a campfire grill for 30 to 40 minutes.

Or place foil packet in covered grill on medium-low heat for 20 minutes.

Foil-Wrapped Vegetables

Sliced carrots, corn cut from the cob, sliced mushrooms, sliced onions, sliced green peppers, sliced or diced white or sweet potatoes, shelled peas, and sliced squash may all be foil-wrapped and cooked on the grill. Season them with plenty of butter and with salt and pepper before wrapping. If desired, vegetables may also be cooked in combinations. Onions and potatoes, corn and green peppers, and peas and mushrooms are good together.

To cook vegetables in ashes, first spray the foil with non-stick cooking spray. Wrap the vegetables securely in heavy duty aluminum foil, then place in or around the ashes. Turn once or twice during the cooking. Using a long pronged fork, test for doneness by piercing through the foil.

Vegetables

Roasted Corn

Husk corn, brush with butter, sprinkle each with garlic or onion salt and wrap in foil before roasting. Turn occasionally during the cooking. Corn will take 10 to 15 minutes or longer. Another method of roasting corn is in the husks: Peel back husks, remove silk with a brush, replace husks, and wire or tie ends. Soak in cold water for half an hour before roasting in or around the ashes.

Roasted Onions

Wrap whole peeled or unpeeled onions in foil, and roast until fork tender. Serve with butter.

Roasted Potatoes

Wrap unpeeled potatoes in foil and roast until fork tender. Or, if you like a hard, blackened skin, roast potatoes without wrapping. Cook potatoes until tender, and turn during the cooking. They will take from 30 to 60 minutes. Serve with plenty of butter, or with sour cream and chives.

Roasted Sweet Potatoes

Cook exactly as directed for white potatoes, but serve with butter and brown sugar.

Spicy Potatoes

6 medium potatoes, washed and chopped
1 bell pepper, chopped
1 onion, chopped
2 tablespoons Molly McButter
1 teaspoon seasoned salt
1/2 teaspoon garlic powder
Heavy duty aluminum foil – 2 pieces 18" x 24"

Spray the foil with non-stick cooking spray. In the center of each foil, place the 1/2 of the potatoes, pepper, and onion. Sprinkle with the McButter, seasoned salt and garlic powder. Mix all ingredients carefully.

Fold the foil loosely to form a tent packet, folding and crimping seams tightly. Grill until the potatoes are tender. Yield: 8 servings.

COOKING

Place foil packet on hot coals or a campfire grill for 55 to 60 minutes.

Or place foil packet in covered grill on medium-low heat for 35 to 45 minutes.

Fire Roasted Broccoli

1 lb. broccoli florets
2 garlic cloves, sliced
2 tablespoons extra-virgin olive oil
1/4 teaspoon red pepper
1/2 teaspoon sea salt
Heavy duty aluminum foil – 18" x 24"

Wash broccoli and separate into florets. Combine all ingredients except broccoli in a bowl, then add broccoli and toss until mixed well. Place broccoli in a single layer on the foil.

Fold the foil loosely to form a tent packet, folding and crimping seams tightly. Cook until tender.

COOKING

Place foil packet on hot coals or a campfire grill for 20 minutes.

Or place foil packet on uncovered grill on medium-low heat for 10 minutes.

Sweet Potatoes with Cran-Apples

2 red apples
4 medium sweet potatoes
1/2 cup dried cranberries
1/2 cup brown sugar, packed
4 tablespoons margarine, melted
1 teaspoon ground cinnamon
Heavy duty aluminum foil – 18" x 24"

Core the apples and slice them thinly into rings. Peel the sweet potatoes and cut into 1/4-inch slices. Spray the foil with non-stick cooking spray. Place the apples, sweet potatoes and cranberries in the center of the foil. Sprinkle with brown sugar. Combine margarine and cinnamon; drizzle over brown sugar.

Fold the foil loosely to form a tent packet, folding and crimping seams tightly. Cook until sweet potatoes are tender. Yield: 4 servings.

COOKING

Place foil packet on hot coals or a campfire grill for 35 to 45 minutes.

Or place foil packet in covered grill on medium-low heat for 20 to 25 minutes.

Fresh Vegetables on the Grill

3 medium carrots, halved lengthwise
3 large potatoes, quartered lengthwise
3 medium zucchini, quartered lengthwise
1/3 cup vegetable oil
1 1/2 teaspoons garlic powder
1/2 teaspoon salt
1/4 teaspoon pepper
1/8 teaspoon cayenne pepper
Heavy duty aluminum foil - 18" x 24"

Spray the foil with non-stick cooking spray. In a small bowl, combine oil, garlic powder, salt, pepper and cayenne pepper. Put vegetables in a single layer on the foil. Brush the oil mixture over vegetables.

Fold the foil loosely to form a tent packet, folding and crimping seams tightly.

Rotate packets 1/2 turn every 10 minutes and cook using one of the options below or until vegetables are tender. Yield: 6 servings.

COOKING

Place foil packet on hot coals or a campfire grill for 35 to 45 minutes.

Or place foil packet in covered grill on medium-low heat for 20 to 25 minutes.

Roasted Corn on the Cob

4 ears of corn
1/4 cup barbecue sauce
1/4 cup butter, melted
Salt and pepper to taste
Heavy duty aluminum foil – 4 pieces 18" x 18"

Husk corn, remove silk and place each ear on a square of foil. Mix the barbecue sauce and butter together. Brush each corn with butter mixture; season with salt and pepper.

Bring foil up over corn and seal lengthwise edges with a double fold. Twist or crimp ends to secure. Cook until corn is tender.

COOKING

Place foil packet on hot coals or a campfire grill for 40 to 50 minutes.

Or place foil packet in covered grill on medium-low heat for 30 to 35 minutes.

Campfire Foil Onions

4 onions
4 beef bouillon cubes
4 teaspoons butter
Salt and pepper to taste
Heavy duty aluminum foil – 4 pieces 18" x 18"

Using an apple corer, make a hole in each onion. Place one onion on each piece of foil. Place 1 bouillon cube and 1 teaspoon butter in each onion. Sprinkle with salt and pepper.

 Wrap foil loosely around onions. Cook using one of the options below. Yield: 4 servings.

COOKING

Place foil packet on hot coals or a campfire grill for 45 minutes.

Or place foil packet in covered grill on medium-low heat for 25 to 30 minutes.

Grilled Potato Slices

4 medium potatoes
1 onion
1 chicken bouillon cube
4 tablespoons butter
1/3 cup cheddar cheese, shredded
1 tablespoon Worcestershire sauce
1 tablespoon parsley
Salt and pepper to taste
Heavy duty aluminum foil – 18" x 24"

Peel and thinly slice potatoes. Cut the onion into slices. Dissolve the bouillon cube in 1/3 cup of hot water.

Spray foil with non-stick cooking spray. Place the onion and potatoes in the center of the foil. Add slices of butter on top of the potatoes. Mix the cheese, Worcestershire sauce and parsley together and add on top of the butter. Sprinkle with salt and pepper. Fold up the sides of the foil to make a bowl and add the hot water with dissolved bouillon cube.

Fold the foil loosely to form a tent packet, folding and crimping seams tightly. Grill until potatoes are tender.

COOKING

Place foil packet on hot coals or a campfire grill for 45 to 60 minutes.

Or place foil packet in covered grill on medium-low heat for 35 to 45 minutes.

Foil Packet Veggies

1 purple onion, sliced
1 cup snow peas, in pods
1 green bell pepper, sliced
3 carrots, cut into strips
1 teaspoon basil
1 garlic clove, chopped
Salt and pepper to taste
2 tablespoons olive oil
Heavy duty aluminum foil – 18" x 20"

Spray foil with non-stick cooking spray. Place vegetables in the center of foil and sprinkle with basil, garlic, salt and pepper. Drizzle olive oil over vegetables.

Fold the foil loosely to form a tent packet, folding and crimping seams tightly. Place the veggie packet on grill or coals. Cook using one of the options below. Yield: 2 servings.

COOKING

Place foil packet on hot coals or a campfire grill for 22 to 30 minutes.

Or place foil packet in covered grill on top rack on medium-low heat for 10 to 15 minutes.

Parmesan Potatoes

4 large potatoes
1 onion, diced
1 teaspoon garlic salt
1 teaspoon salt
1/4 teaspoon black pepper
1/2 cup Parmesan cheese, shredded
4 tablespoons butter
Heavy duty aluminum foil – 18" x 24"

Spray the foil with non-stick cooking spray. Peel and cut potatoes into French fry style slices. Place potatoes in the center of the foil; sprinkle with garlic salt, diced onion and salt and pepper. Top with Parmesan cheese and dots of butter.

Fold the foil loosely to form a tent packet, folding and crimping seams tightly. Cook over medium-low heat, rotating packet 1/2 turn occasionally. Yield: 4 servings.

COOKING

Place foil packet on hot coals or a campfire grill for 45 to 60 minutes.

Or place foil packet in covered grill on medium-low heat for 35 to 45 minutes.

Corn with Herbs

8 ears sweet corn, husked
1/2 cup margarine, softened
2 tablespoons parsley
2 tablespoons fresh chives, minced
1/2 teaspoon salt
1 teaspoon dried thyme
1/4 teaspoon cayenne pepper
Heavy duty aluminum foil – 8 pieces 18" x 12"

In a small bowl, combine margarine, parsley, chives, salt, thyme and pepper. Spread 1 tablespoon of mixture over each ear of corn.

Wrap each corn individually in foil. Grill, turning occasionally, until corn is tender. Yield: 8 servings.

COOKING

Place foil packet on hot coals or a campfire grill for 40 to 50 minutes.

Or place foil packet in covered grill on medium-low heat for 30 to 35 minutes.

Grilled Mushrooms

1 lb. Portobello mushrooms
2 tablespoons rosemary
2 tablespoons thyme
2 tablespoons sage
1 tablespoon mint
3 cloves of garlic, thinly chopped
3 tablespoons olive oil, extra virgin
Salt and pepper to taste
Heavy duty aluminum foil – 4 pieces 18" x 12"

Clean the mushrooms and cut into 1/2" thick slices. Spray the foil with non-stick cooking spray. In a bowl, combine the mushrooms, rosemary, thyme, sage, mint, garlic, 2 tablespoons olive oil and salt and pepper; blend well. Place equal portions of mushrooms on each foil square.

Fold the foil loosely to form a tent packet, folding and crimping seams tightly. Mushrooms should be juicy and tender when done. Great as a side dish or served on top of a juicy steak.

COOKING

Place foil packet on hot coals or a campfire grill for 20 to 25 minutes.

Or place foil packet in covered grill on medium-low heat for 15 to 20 minutes.

Sweet Potato Grillers

2 sweet potatoes, peeled and cut into 1-inch pieces
1 yellow bell pepper
1 tablespoon honey
2 tablespoons butter, melted
1/2 teaspoon seasoned salt
Heavy duty aluminum foil – 18" x 24"

Spray the foil with non-stick cooking spray. Combine honey, butter and salt; drizzle over potatoes, mix well. Place potatoes on the center of the foil. Cut the bell pepper into slices and add to the foil.

Fold the foil loosely to form a tent packet, folding and crimping seams tightly. Potatoes should be tender when done. Yield: 2 servings.

COOKING

Place foil packet on hot coals or a campfire grill for 30 to 40 minutes.

Or place foil packet in covered grill on medium-low heat for 15 to 20 minutes.

Scalloped Potatoes

4 large baking potatoes, sliced thin
1 can condensed cream of mushroom soup
1 onion, sliced thin
1 cup cheddar cheese, shredded
Salt to taste
Heavy duty aluminium foil – 4 pieces 18" x 18"

Spray foil with cooking spray. On each piece of foil, place a spoonful of cream of mushroom soup, a layer of sliced potatoes, a layer of onion and a layer of cheese. Then another layer of soup, potatoes, cheese and onion. Sprinkle with a little salt.

Fold the foil loosely to form a tent packet, folding and crimping seams tightly. Cook until potatoes are tender, using one of the options below, rotating packet 1/2 turn at half done. Yield: 4 servings.

COOKING

Place foil packet on hot coals or a campfire grill for 55 to 60 minutes.

Or place foil packet in covered grill on medium-low heat for 25 to 30 minutes.

Foil-Baked Tomatoes

6 medium firm tomatoes
1 onion, thinly sliced
Salt and pepper to taste
Heavy duty aluminium foil – 6 pieces 18" x 12"

Remove stem ends from tomatoes and cut in half crosswise.
Sprinkle with salt and pepper to taste. Place onion slices
between tomato halves and secure with wooden picks.
Spray the foil with non-stick cooking spray.

Wrap tomatoes individually in heavy-duty aluminum
foil. Grill packets until hot. Yield: 6 servings.

COOKING

Place foil packet on hot coals or a campfire grill for
22 to 30 minutes.

Or place foil packet in covered grill on medium-low
heat for 10 to 15 minutes.

Creamy Beans

2 cans green beans, 16 oz. each, drained
1 package cream cheese, 3 oz., cubed
Heavy duty aluminium foil – 4 pieces 18" x 24"

Spray the foil with non-stick cooking spray. Combine beans with cream cheese. Place in the center of the foil and season with salt and pepper.

Fold the foil tightly to form a flat packet with securely crimped seams. Cook using one of the options below, turning foil packet over once while cooking. Yield: 4 to 5 servings.

COOKING

Place foil packet on hot coals or a campfire grill for 25 to 40 minutes.

Or place foil packet in covered grill on medium-low heat for 18 to 22 minutes.

Grilled Acorn Squash

3 medium acorn squash
2 tablespoons margarine
2 tablespoons brown sugar
2 tablespoons water
1 apple, peeled and cut into wedges
Heavy duty aluminium foil – 6 pieces 18" x 24"

Cut squash in half and remove seeds. Prick the inside with a fork; season with salt and pepper. To each squash half, add 1 teaspoon each of margarine, sugar, and water. Top the squash off with apple pieces.

Wrap each half, cut side up, in heavy foil; seal.

Place squash, cut side up, on grill. Close hood and cook until squash is done. Open packets; stir to fluff squash. Top with more brown sugar. Yield: 6 servings.

COOKING

Place foil packet in covered grill on medium-low heat for 50 to 60 minutes.

Foiled French Fries

1 package frozen French-fried potatoes, 24 oz.
1/2 cup shredded Parmesan cheese
1 teaspoon dried basil, crushed
1 teaspoon salt
Heavy duty aluminium foil – 6 pieces 18" x 12"

Spray the foil with non-stick cooking spray. Divide potatoes evenly on the pieces of foil. Mix cheese, basil, and salt; sprinkle on top of the potatoes.

Fold the foil tightly to form a flat packet with securely crimped seams. Cook using one of the options below, turning occasionally. Yield: 6 servings.

COOKING

Place foil packet on hot coals or a campfire grill for 25 minutes.

Or place foil packet in covered grill on medium-low heat for 15 minutes.

Herbed Zucchini

4 medium zucchini
2 medium tomatoes
2 tablespoons onion, minced
1 teaspoon salt
3/4 teaspoon dried oregano, crushed
1 tablespoon butter
Heavy duty aluminium foil – 18" x 24"

Spray the foil with non-stick cooking spray. Cut the zucchini into 1/2 inch slices and the tomatoes into large wedges. Place zucchini slices in the center of the foil. Top with tomatoes; sprinkle with onion, salt, and oregano. Dot with butter.

Fold the foil loosely to form a tent packet, folding and crimping seams tightly. Cook until zucchini is tender, turning packet once. Yield: 6 to 8 servings.

COOKING

Place foil packet on hot coals or a campfire grill for 35 to 40 minutes.

Or place foil packet in covered grill on medium-low heat for 20 to 25 minutes.

Breakfast

Eggs in Foil

4 eggs
Heavy-duty aluminum foil – 4 pieces 18" x 9"

Make 4 cups by molding foil around the bottom of a 1 lb. can or about 3" in diameter. Crack an egg into each foil cup. Cook directly on medium coals until done.

COOKING

Place foil packet on hot coals or a campfire grill for 15 to 20 minutes.

Or place foil packet in covered grill on medium-low heat for 15 to 20 minutes.

Bacon, Egg & Cheese Muffin

2 English muffins
2 slices of ham, cooked
2 slices of bacon, cooked
2 eggs
2 slices of American or pepper jack cheese
Heavy duty aluminum foil – 2 pieces 18" x 20"

Place an English muffin in the center of each piece of foil, top it with ham and cooked bacon. Top each with a raw egg.

Seal foil packet leaving some room at top. Place about 4 inches from medium coals. Top with cheese when egg is cooked. Yield: 2 servings.

COOKING

Place foil packet on hot coals or a campfire grill for 20 to 25 minutes.

Or place foil packet on uncovered grill on medium-low heat for 20 to 25 minutes.

Bogota Bread Omelet

4 slices white bread, cubed
1/2 cup milk
3 eggs, beaten
1/2 teaspoon sugar
2 tablespoons vegetable oil
Heavy duty aluminum foil

Coat a shallow, heat-resistant casserole dish or heavy metal pan with the oil. Place the bread and milk in the dish or pan and wait until the bread has completed soaked up the milk. Beat eggs with sugar and pour over bread. Make a tent of foil on top of dish or pan to enclose omelet.

Place cooking grill 4 to 6 inches above bed of medium-glowing coals. Cook 12 to 14 minutes and check. When toothpick comes out clean, slice into wedges and serve with jelly or syrup and mounds of fresh fruit. Yield: 6 servings.

COOKING

Place foil packet on hot coals or a campfire grill for 12 to 14 minutes.

Or place foil packet on uncovered grill on medium-low heat for 12 to 14 minutes.

Breakfast Hole in One

4 slices of bacon
4 slices Texas toast or thick sliced French bread
4 eggs
Heavy duty aluminum foil – 4 pieces 18" x 18"

In the center of each piece of foil, lay one slice of bacon. Create a hole in the center of each slice of bread and lay the bread on top of the bacon. Crack an egg into the hole in the bread on each piece of foil.

Fold the foil loosely to form a tent packet, folding and crimping seams tightly. Cook using one of the options below. Yield: 4 servings.

COOKING

Place foil packet in covered grill on medium-low heat for 8 to 10 minutes.

SMORES!

DESSERT
FOIL
PACKETS

Dessert

Honey Glazed Pineapple

1 fresh pineapple, peeled, cored, and cut in spears or rings
3 to 4 tablespoons honey
1/4 cup dark rum (optional)
Heavy duty aluminum foil – 18" x 24"

Place pineapple in center of the foil. Drizzle honey and rum, if desired, over fruit.

Bring edges of foil up and over to seal. Cook using one of the options below or until heated through. Serve with ham or barbecued pork. Yield: 4 to 6 servings.

COOKING

Place foil packet on hot coals or a campfire grill for 15 to 20 minutes.

Or place foil packet in covered grill on medium-low heat for 8 to 10 minutes.

Hawaiian Rum Oranges

4 seedless oranges
2 tablespoons brown sugar
1/2 teaspoon ground cinnamon
1/3 cup light rum
2 tablespoons butter
Heavy duty aluminum foil – 4 pieces 18" x 12"

Peel oranges and separate into sections. Place sections from each orange in the center of a piece of foil. Combine sugar and cinnamon; sprinkle over each orange. Pour 1/4 of the rum on each of the oranges; dot with butter.

Fold foil around oranges and seal securely. Cook oranges until hot. Yield: 4 servings.

COOKING

Place foil packet on hot coals or a campfire grill for 18 to 25 minutes.

Or place foil packet in covered grill on medium-low heat for 10 to 12 minutes.

Foil-Wrapped Fruits

To cook fruits in ashes, first wrap them securely in heavy duty aluminum foil, then place in or around the ashes. Turn once or twice during the cooking. Using a long pronged fork, test to see if done by piercing through the foil.

Fruits

Roasted Apples

Core apples and fill holes with sugar and a piece of butter, also cinnamon or nutmeg, if desired. Wrap in foil and cook on hot coals for 30 minutes, or until fork tender.

Roasted Bananas

Wrap unpeeled bananas in foil. Or peel, dip in melted butter, and sprinkle with sugar before wrapping. Cook on hot coals for 30 minutes.

Roasted Peaches

Peel and cut in slices. Season with butter and brown sugar. Wrap in foil and cook on hot coals for 30 minutes.

Roasted Pears

Peel and slice; season with butter, sugar, and ginger, or add slivered candied ginger. Wrap in foil and cook on hot coals for 30 minutes.

Roasted Pineapple

Use pineapple chunks. Season with butter and sugar. Wrap in foil and cook on hot coals for 30 minutes.

COOKING

Place foil packet on hot coals or a campfire grill for 30 minutes.

Or place foil packet in covered grill on medium-low heat for 18 minutes.

Apple Crisp (On the Grill)

This recipe works well when camping because the dry ingredients can be premeasured and kept in 2 Ziploc bags until ready to make the apple crisp.

8 to 10 cups sliced apples
1 cup sugar
1 teaspoon cinnamon
2 tablespoons flour

1/2 cup butter
1 cup brown sugar
1/2 cup + 2 tablespoons flour
1 cup old-fashioned oats
1/2 teaspoon salt
Heavy duty aluminum foil – 2 pieces 18" x 24"

Spray each piece of foil with cooking spray. Place half the apples on each piece of foil. Combine the sugar, cinnamon and 2 tablespoons flour. Sprinkle each set of apples with half the sugar mixture. Combine the remaining ingredients and crumb as for a pie crust. Sprinkle over the top of the apples.

Fold the foil tightly to form a flat packet, crimping seams tightly. Cook until fork tender.

COOKING

Cook in covered grill on medium-low heat for 20 to 25 minutes.

Cinnamon Stuffed Apples

4 large baking apples
1/2 cup raisins
1/2 cup water
2 tablespoons walnuts, chopped
2 tablespoons brown sugar
2 tablespoons maraschino cherries, chopped
1 teaspoon ground cinnamon
1/8 teaspoon ground cloves
1/8 teaspoon ground nutmeg
2 tablespoons margarine
Heavy duty aluminum foil – 4 pieces 18" x 12"

Core apples, leaving just a little of the center core at the bottom (as a floor). Enlarge each opening slightly; do not peel. Spray foil with non-stick cooking spray. Place each apple on a piece of foil.

Mix together raisins, water, walnuts, brown sugar, cherries, cinnamon, cloves, and nutmeg. Divide mixture 4 ways into the cavities of the apples. Dot with margarine.

Bring foil up around apples; seal loosely. Apples are done when they are fork tender. Yield: 4 servings.

COOKING

Place foil packet on hot coals or a campfire grill for 35 to 45 minutes or until apples are tender.

Or place foil packet in covered grill on medium-low heat for 20 to 25 minutes or until apples are tender.

S'Mores in Foil

4 graham crackers, broken in half into 8 squares
3/4 cup semi-sweet chocolate chunks or a piece of chocolate candy bar
4 large marshmallows
Heavy duty aluminum foil – 4 pieces 18" x 12"

Place a graham cracker square on each foil, then add chocolate chunks followed by a large marshmallow. Add the other graham cracker square on top and wrap the foil tightly.

Cook until marshmallows and chocolate are melted.

COOKING

Place foil packet on hot coals or a campfire grill for 4 to 5 minutes.

Or place foil packet on uncovered grill on low heat for 4 to 5 minutes.

Miscellaneous

Bits and Pieces Bread

1 loaf garlic bread
1/2 cup margarine
3 teaspoons garlic powder
1 small onion, chopped
1/4 green pepper, chopped
1 package pepperoni
2 cups shredded pepper jack or mozzarella cheese
Heavy duty aluminum foil – 18" x 24"

Place bread on its side and cut in half lengthwise. Melt margarine and mix with garlic powder; butter both inside sections of the bread with the garlic margarine mix. Spread the onions and green peppers, pepperoni and cheese on one portion of the bread. Place the other bread portion on top.

Wrap in foil and cook until cheese is melted.

COOKING

Place foil packet on hot coals or a campfire grill for 20 to 30 minutes.

Or place foil packet in covered grill on medium-low heat for 15 to 20 minutes.

Hot Turkey Buns

2 cups cooked turkey, diced
1/2 cup celery, finely diced
4 tablespoons green pepper, chopped
3 small green onions, chopped
1/4 cup mayonnaise
1/2 teaspoon salt
1 to 1 1/2 cups shredded Cheddar cheese
12 hamburger buns
Heavy duty aluminum foil – 12 pieces 18" x 12"

In a bowl, mix all ingredients together except for buns. Split the buns and fill with turkey mixture. Mixture should be very dry.

Wrap in foil, seal tightly. Cook using one of the options below until the cheese melts. Yield: 12 servings.

COOKING

Place foil packet on hot coals or a campfire grill for 20 to 25 minutes.

Or place foil packet in covered grill on medium-low heat for 12 to 15 minutes.

Herbed Italian Bread

1 loaf Italian bread (12 to 14 inches long)
1/4 lb. soft butter or margarine
1 teaspoon parsley flakes
1/4 teaspoon oregano
1 clove garlic, crushed
4 tablespoons shredded Parmesan cheese
Heavy duty aluminum foil – 18" x 24"

Cut bread diagonally in 3/4-inch slices, almost but not quite through the bottom crust. Combine butter or margarine with parsley flakes, oregano, garlic and spread on both sides of each bread slice.

Place bread in center of foil, shaping the foil around sides. Combine any remaining butter mixture with Parmesan cheese and spread on top of loaf. Heat bread until warm using one of the options below.

COOKING

Place foil packet on hot coals or a campfire grill for 20 to 25 minutes.

Or place foil packet in covered grill on medium-low heat for 15 minutes.

Veggie Burgers

4 frozen vegetarian burger patties
2 cups fresh mushrooms, cut in half
1 can green beans, 15 oz.
1/2 red bell pepper, cut into strips
1 onion, cut into wedges
1/2 cup honey mustard barbecue sauce
Heavy duty aluminum foil – 4 pieces 18" x 12"

Spray each foil with non-stick cooking spray. Combine mushrooms, bell pepper, green beans, onion wedges and barbecue sauce. Place equal portions of mushroom mixture on each foil piece. Place a veggie burger patty on top of mushrooms.

Fold the foil loosely to form a tent packet, folding and crimping seams tightly. Cook using one of the options below or until patty is hot. Yield: 4 servings.

COOKING

Place foil packet on hot coals or a campfire grill for 25 to 40 minutes.

Or place foil packet in covered grill on medium-low heat for 18 to 22 minutes.

Turkey Hobo Dinner

1 1/2 cups diced or 4 slices 1/2" thick turkey ham
1 cup frozen corn
4 tablespoons pimento cheese spread
Heavy duty aluminum foil - 4 pieces 18" x 12"

Place 1 slice of turkey ham or 1/4 of the diced ham in the center of each piece of foil. To each piece of foil, add 1/4 cup corn and 1 rounded tablespoon of pimento cheese on top of the meat.

Fold the foil loosely to form a tent packet, folding and crimping seams tightly. Cook using one of the options below, rotating packet 1/2 turn occasionally. Yield: 4 servings.

COOKING

Place foil packet on hot coals or a campfire grill for 25 to 30 minutes.

Or place foil packet in covered grill on medium-low heat for 15 minutes.

149

Pizza Bread

1 loaf Vienna bread (or other Italian bread)
1/2 cup mushrooms, sliced
1/2 cup green peppers
1 can sliced black olives, 2.25 oz.
1 package pepperoni
1 package shredded Swiss or mozzarella cheese, 10 oz.

1/2 cup butter, melted
1 tablespoon minced onion
1/2 teaspoon seasoned salt
1/2 teaspoon lemon juice
1/2 teaspoon dry mustard
1/2 teaspoon garlic powder
1 tablespoons poppy seeds (optional)
Heavy duty aluminum foil – 18" x 24"

Slice Vienna bread diagonally; turn and slice diagonally the other way to crisscross like an "X". Stuff with mushrooms, green peppers, black olives, pepperoni and cheese.

Mix together butter, onion, seasoned salt, lemon juice, dry mustard, garlic powder and poppy seeds. Pour mixture over stuffed bread.

Wrap bread tightly in foil. Cook using one of the options below until the cheese is melted.

COOKING

Place foil packet on hot coals or a campfire grill for 20 to 30 minutes.

Or place foil packet in covered grill on medium-low heat for 15 to 20 minutes.

Popcorn in Foil

1 tablespoon vegetable oil
1/4 cup popcorn kernels
Salt to taste
Disposable pie pan
Heavy duty aluminum foil - 18" x 24"

Pour the oil in the pie pan and add popcorn kernels. Make a tent out of foil on top of the pie pan by wrapping one edge around the edges of the pie pan and the other edge gathered at the very top to make a tent. Seal edges well. Attach the top of the foil to a long stick with a piece of string. Cook on high heat, shaking constantly, about 8 minutes or until popping stops. Add salt to taste.

Note: If a pie pan is not available, this can be accomplished by just using foil. Make sure the foil is tent-like so the popcorn can pop. Tie a string to a corner of the foil packet and attach the string to a long stick. Shake over fire until all is popped.

COOKING

Shake foil packet over a campfire for 8 minutes or until popping stops.

Grilled Cheese Rolls

1 package cream cheese, 3 oz., softened
1/2 cup shredded cheddar cheese
2 tablespoons green onion, chopped
1 tablespoon milk
2 teaspoons Dijon-style mustard
12 dinner rolls
Heavy duty aluminum foil – 18" x 24"

In a bowl, combine cream cheese, cheddar cheese, green onion, milk and mustard. Split each dinner roll in half horizontally. Spread part of the cheese mixture in each roll; reassemble the rolls.

Wrap rolls loosely in heavy foil, crimping seams tightly. Cook until hot, turning once. Yield: 12 rolls.

COOKING

Place foil packet on hot coals or a campfire grill for 15 to 18 minutes.

Or place foil packet in covered grill on low heat for 10 minutes.

Other books by Bonnie Scott

100 Easy Camping Recipes

Fish & Game Cookbook

Pies and Mini Pies

100 Easy Recipes in Jars

Soups, Sandwiches and Wraps

Slow Cooker Comfort Foods

Cookie Indulgence: 150 Easy Cookie Recipes

Holiday Recipes

All titles available in Paperback and Kindle versions at Amazon.com

Also visit our website for more recipes and freebies:

www.CampingFreebies.com

Photo credits:

Photos by filo/Photos.com
and AGL Photo productions

Graphics by Cheryl Seslar

Made in the USA
Middletown, DE
22 May 2016